in and MANY VARIOUS ways

EXPLORATIONS
IN SERMONIC FORM

MARK WILLIAM RADECKE

IN MANY AND VARIOUS WAYS

5806/ISBN 0-89536-721-1

To my loving wife,
Lee

Table of Contents

Introduction

*There is no ideal or standard form which every sermon should take.
The sermon is not a species with fixed and invariable characteristics,
as the form of the violet, the lily, the leaf of the red oak, the twig
of the weeping willow is fixed. There is no preexistent mold into which
the substance of thought must be poured in order to make a sermon.*
— H. Grady Davis — Design For Preaching[1]

Substance, form, and function: every sermon has all three. And
all who mount the pulpit have wrestled, some long and hard and
others not enough, with their sermon's substance. Some will even
have considered its intended function: what they want the sermon
to *do* in the lives of the hearers. But little thought will likely have
been given to the form of the sermon and its relationship to
substance and function.

This is not to say that the preacher's task is to invent or borrow
a form and then proceed to fill it with substance as one would find
a bucket or a jar and fill it with water. The relationship between form
and substance is far more intricate and intimate. As the sermon's
substance *takes shape* in the preacher's mind, the preacher must
attend to both the quality of the substance and the appropriateness
of the form in light of the intended function. It simply will not do
to sit down ahead of time and say, "Whatever the content, next Sunday's sermon will have three points and a poem" (or two points and
a deathbed scene). Only when form grows out of and is virtually
demanded by the developing substance and intended function will
the sermon be a unity, at one with itself, better able to perform that
function.

Why is form so vitally important? A few biblical examples: would
the Story of the Creation and Fall in Genesis 2 and 3 have its
evocative impact if it were cast in the form of a series of intellectual propositions? Would the Song of the Vineyard (Isaiah 5:1-7) have
the power to touch and wound hard hearts if it assumed the form
of an oracle of doom rather than a parabolic song about a faithless
lover? Or, dealing with the same basic thought: is Paul's direct,
polemic and epistolary way of talking about justification by faith not
appropriate to his audience and function even as is Jesus' way of
talking about justification in the Parable of the Pharisee and the
Publican (Luke 18) appropriate to his? In each case, the form is called

[1] Fortress Press, Philadelphia, p. 8.

8

for by the substance and the intended function among a specific group of hearers. The preacher who is a faithful student of the scriptures will learn from them not only *what* to say, but *how* to say it as well.

Yet there are hazards: being inventive for inventiveness' sake, calling attention not to the proclaimed word, but to the cleverness of the preacher. Or the false notion that one must somehow "find" or "invent" or "come up with" a new and unique form each week. The preacher does well to remember that substance, form and function comprise a unity and that substance and function will suggest and call for an appropriate form in the process of preparation. Part of the preacher's task is to attend to such suggestions and calls and heed them.

Further, one would be ill advised simply to spring new forms on a congregation unaware. In most of the sermons in this volume, I alerted the congregation to the fact that what was to follow would be a little different. Elizabeth Achtemeier's *caveat* is to the point:

> There must be some understanding and expectation of experimental forms created in the congregation before those forms can be used with any effectiveness whatsoever. Otherwise, the members of the church are alienated, and the unchurched see nothing about the body of Christ which is different from the expressions of the culture around them.[2]

Honest, reliable, and candid parishioners are invaluable in helping the preacher gauge whether substantially different forms are indeed achieving their desired effect among the hearers.

All that harsh stuff having been said, we may turn to the serendipitous side of this whole venture. We take the craft of preaching seriously, yet we acknowledge with St. Paul that preaching is foolishness, lest we take ourselves too seriously.

From the practical standpoint, coaxing out appropriate sermonic forms frees the preacher from the constraints of saying the same things the same way week in and week out — the old saying, "Give a kid a hammer and he'll treat the whole world as if it were a nail." Such formal variations also invite and encourage the listeners to tune in more closely, for the change in form puts them on the alert to the possibility that they might hear something they've not heard before, at least not quite that way.

---

[2]Elizabeth Achtemeier, *Creative Preaching* (Nashville: Abingdon, 1980), p. 77.

In the following pages, I share with you some of my explorations in sermonic form and refer you to your own creativity, sensitivity, and imagination in heeding the call to cast your sermons in appropriate new forms.

Per evangelica dicta
Deleantur nostra delicta.[3]

Thanks are due to a number of people: to Linda Akers who labored over virtually illegible manuscripts; to Tom Ridenhour who read and reacted to the work; and to the people of Christ Lutheran Church, Roanoke, whose partnership in the gospel makes preaching a delight.

---

[3] "May our sins be blotted out by the words of the gospel."

Letter to a Friend

Fred B. Craddock has suggested that preachers give their people opportunity to "overhear" the gospel. He builds on Søren Kierkegaard's discussion of indirect communication and suggests that people participate more deeply in the sermon when it is indirectly communicated than when it is directly proclaimed.[1]

While I am not ready to discard direct proclamation altogether, I do accept Craddock's suggestion. Eavesdropping is always exciting. So is reading other people's mail, and that is what I allowed my congregation to do when I preached "The Acoustical Phenomenon."

This sermonic form or style does have one peculiar drawback: eye contact, so vital in direct address, is actually counter-productive in reading the letter aloud to the congregation. It breaks the "fourth wall" that separates letter writer and addressee from the eavesdropping listeners. Indeed, it reminds them of their clandestine activity and forces a shift from the indirect to the direct mode.

In preaching this sermon, I began by reading the "inside address" and never once looked up from the manuscript. And yes, for the sake of honesty, I mailed it to the addressee.

---

[1]Fred B. Craddock, *Overhearing the Gospel* (Nashville: Abingdon, 1978).

The Acoustical Phenomenon

Matthew 7:15-29
Deuteronomy 11:18-28

The Rev. Dr. Thomas Ridenhour
Professor of the Art of Preaching
Lutheran Theological Seminary
Gettysburg, PA 17325

Dear Tom:

You told me there would be times like this. Times when a sermon just wouldn't come. Like a baseball player in a batting slump — no matter how many times he's hit the ball before, comes the time he just can't make it to first base.

Well, it's taken a few years, but it finally happened to me. It is now Saturday morning; I just got back from an eight-day vacation visiting friends and relatives in five states and the District of Columbia. I'm rested, invigorated, glad to be back — and I've got to preach tomorrow morning.

Before I left, I wrote half a sermon — or half wrote a sermon, I'm not sure which — and felt pretty good about leaving and finishing it up when I got back. I even had the secretary type up what I'd already written.

When I came back to the office this morning, I picked it up and read it. At this moment, it is lying crumpled up around my feet.

Oh, it was scholarly, erudite, decent prose, and all that good stuff. It's just that it didn't have anything to do with anything. At least nothing real. It was a very careful academic examination of how Jesus could demand all the things he demands in the Sermon on the Mount — loving your enemies, turning the other cheek, doing his Father's will and not just saying "Lord, Lord," bringing forth good fruits, and so on — and still justify us by faith and not by works.

Abstract, rarified God talk, church talk, very safe, very unthreatening and just so not the gospel, the good news you so well taught me I'm supposed to preach shortly after sun-up tomorrow.

That sermon lying on the floor was what I call a Muzak Sermon. In the background, it goes on and on, not really meant to be listened to, while the father in the ninth pew plays Tic-Tac-Toe with his daughter, six or so people stare out the window silently wondering how their lives could possibly get more screwed up than they already are, and somebody else tries hard to remember if she cut the stove off before she left the house. And nobody hears anything good except maybe a harmless little introductory joke and they certainly don't hear anything new, so since the gospel is always good and ever new, they hear no gospel; they are sent empty away and it's my fault.

At least at the early service we'll celebrate Communion — the visible Word of Gospel. That takes some of the pressure off. About a year and a half ago, after I'd preached my worst sermon ever, a pastor who worships here said to me, "You know, sermons like that are excellent arguments for weekly Communion. At least then, if you don't get fed from the pulpit, you know you'll get fed at the altar." God bless him, I couldn't agree more. Maybe someday — and I hope it's soon — we'll all stop pretending we don't need to commune intimately with God and each other every Lord's Day.

So here I sit, wondering what to do with some very difficult Bible passages. One from Deuteronomy: "Behold, I set before you today a blessing and a curse — the blessing if you obey the commandments of the Lord and the curse if you do not obey." And another from the Sermon on the Mount: Jesus' hard and harsh words about demolished beach houses, trees tossed into the fire, and the denial that calling him "Lord, Lord" and doing mighty works in his name guarantees a ticket into his Father's Kingdom.

The second lesson does provide a convenient escape route. It's from St. Paul's most Lutheran letter, Romans, and a favorite Lutheran verse at that: "We hold that a man is justified by faith apart from works of the law." I could take out that old Reformation Day sermon and dust it off. But that would be dishonest. It would also be dumb, because I wrote and preached that sermon here two years ago. Not that anybody remembers two-year-old sermons.

I think it was my vacation that did this to me, reminded me that people just don't think theology all the time; are not, by and large, preoccupied with divine blessings and curses, justification, or even entry into the Kingdom of Heaven.

The ones I visited and played and talked with last week are more concerned about the Kingdom of Earth. And I must confess I share their concern. After all, the heart of the gospel is that, in Christ, God brought heaven to earth rather than demanding that earth ascend to heaven. The Kingdom of Heaven — the Kingdom of Earth — both of them belong to God.

I found it interesting last week that a lot of separate conversations eventually got around to the current Congress and Administration and the proposed budget cuts. They ran the gamut from a Head Start Administrator who wonders about the future of that and other children's programs (and consequently his own livelihood) to well-to-do but bitter folks who savor the prospect of dismantling the welfare system. On other fronts one relative doesn't like playing what she considers dishonest little games of office politics; another is disappointed because he's not being promoted as rapidly as he was promised he would be. Then there was news of a friend who lost his three-week-old job because he tends to get arrogant and belligerent when he drinks, which is too often and too much. All in all, your ordinary, everyday conversations.

Not that it was all, or even mostly, bad news or bad times: Jessica shedding her clothes and running through a lawn sprinkler in the altogether; a bushel of steamed crabs in the backyard I grew up in; old friendships renewed and return visits promised; lots of hugs and kisses; one day at a park and another at the National Zoo with little children to the likes of whom the Kingdom definitely belongs.

All of this, I discovered again, is the stuff of life, the hopes, the dreams, the wonder, the laughter, the joys, the happiness, the frustrations, the sorrow, the disappointment, the failures, the fear, the fragility, and all the rest of it. And it is to that stuff that the gospel must speak — check that, it is to that stuff that I as proclaimer of the gospel must speak tomorrow morning if I am to be at all relevant and if the gospel is to be indeed new and good and have anything to do with anything.

The problem, of course, is how to do that, how to preach not like the Scribes but as one with authority, given tomorrow's Bible texts.

I think it must have something — a lot of something — to do with the Promise. The Promise that life with its good stuff and its bad stuff and all that stuff in between that is neither good nor bad — turns out to be far deeper and richer and more purposeful than our efforts alone would make it, especially since our efforts too often tend to make life shallower, meaner, and less purposeful given our freedom and propensity to screw everything up.

The power or the force which makes life deeper and so forth is — in theological terms — grace. And trusting the One who makes it so is faith. Somehow I've got to say that without making God come off as a soft warm fuzzy wuzzy indulgent old grandfather who wouldn't dare demand anything of his people. Or implying that faith is something we can create in ourselves of our own free will and accord. And all this in the framework of blessings and curses, law and gospel.

Of course, the people already know that a whole lot of our misery we bring on ourselves — intentionally choosing disobedience and the curse, intentionally building on a less-than-firm foundation, hearing Christ's words and refusing to do them. So how am I to preach that as *good* news, good news which creates trust and faith which in turn grabs hold of the promise and grace? You're the one who taught me you don't get flowers to grow by pulling on them.

Maybe it does have something to do with what Jesus was saying in those parables. It's not the bad tree's fault that it bears rotten, stunted, evil fruit any more than the good tree can take credit for what sort of fruit it produces. Good trees give good fruit and bad trees don't, and it has usually to do with roots and rain and soil and sunshine — things the tree cannot control.

Or the parable of the two houses — the survival of the house depends not on the strength of the walls or the quality of construction, but where the darned thing's built!

In both cases, the base, the foundation, the roots are critical. And what Jesus calls for is not simply good works, nor even mighty works, nor even mighty works in his name, nor even calling him "personal Lord and Savior," but rather radical, fundamental change, a change of roots, a change of foundations, a change in the essential way life is looked at and thought about and planned for and lived. I wonder how many people will know that the words "root" and "radical" come from the same Latin word "radix."

Somehow I've got to get that across and get across at the same time that such a radical change comes as a gift, like when a gardener transplants a sickly seedling. Somebody says or does something, and the upshot of it is that you can never look at life quite the same way again.

Perhaps the key there is Luther's description of faith as a hearing event, what you said he called "The Acoustical Phenomenon." (I selected that as the sermon title two weeks ago — I ought to work it in somehow.) An acoustical phenomenon because faith comes by hearing Christ's promises of meaning and worth and purpose and fulfillment and love in spite of unloveliness. It is hearing at the very depths of existence, at the root, the foundation. And it is hearing which results in new and renewed roots. A life rooted neither in fear nor fervor for the current Congress and Administration, nor in work, nor in family, nor even in vacations. But life rooted in the Dayspring, the Crucified and Risen Christ, inevitably and naturally producing the good works, the good fruits of obedience — the love of enemies, the turning of the other cheek and all the rest of it — that God fully expects from us.

Maybe then I could say something about our roots being watered by the ever flowing waters of Baptism, our lives strengthened and nourished by Communion.

The whole point, of course, is to get the father and daughter in the ninth pew, the half dozen window gazers, the stove person and all the rest of those beautiful people to know — really know — that God loves them and wants to be the foundation, the root system, the radix of their lives so that they may know his blessings, may know his sure and certain love when the winds of politics and economics and ill fortune blow and beat upon their houses; to know his love so that they might produce the sort of enemy-loving, cheek-turning fruits which he expects and which the world he loves so much so desperately needs.

It'll not be an easy sermon to write, I think. But by the grace of God and the power of his Spirit, perhaps we'll have an Acoustical Phenomenon. Perhaps someone will hear something radically relevant and promising, something faith and fruit producing.

Perhaps.

Blessings (and not curses) to you and thanks for listening.

Your former student and
brother in Christ,

Mark

Narrative

Literature on narrative now abounds. In the simplest terms, it is storytelling, the ancient, indeed, primeval art form. "That Man in My Office" is an attempt to tell the story of a common incident as an (indeed, for this sermon, the) illustration of God's presence and activity in our everyday lives, which illustration grows out of study of and reflection on a specific biblical text.

There is in narrative preaching a question of honesty and integrity. The story I tell is a story of an event in my life, and I relate it so. If it were purely imaginary, I would feel constained to relate it as such. If it happened to an acquaintance or any other third party, again, honesty would dictate that the congregation be so apprised.

That Man in My Office

Mark 9:30-37

I wonder what you would think if I told you that Jesus Christ was in my office within the past few weeks.

Some of you would probably say, "Uh oh, the pressure's finally getting to him. He's hallucinating — just a matter of time before he goes off the deep end."

Others, less skeptical and more pious, might say, "Of course Jesus was in your office; he promised that wherever two or more are gathered in his name he would be there in their midst, and Jesus is faithful to his promises."

Of course he is, but there was nobody else in the office, just him and me, both in the flesh.

He arrived unannounced. Didn't even have the common courtesy to call for an appointment. He just showed up. Linda Akers, the secretary, called me on the intercom to let me know that he was here and was asking to see me. Actually, he was asking to see either Pastor Morgan or me, but Paul wasn't in, so the lot fell on me.

My first reaction — and this may seem strange to you just as it does to me now that I look back on it — was, "Oh, Lord, not today. Not now. I have a sermon and three lesson plans to prepare, reports to get out, phone calls to make, more work than I can say grace over. Why now? Why me?"

But of course, I told her to send him in. I'm not proud of this, but I told her to send him in more out of a sense of obligation and duty and not knowing what else to do than out of a spirit of joy and wonder and anticipation.

I opened my door just as he walked down the hall. The very first thing he did put me on the defensive. He called me "reverend," and I'm always uneasy whenever anyone calls me "reverend."

I tried not to let it show even though I know I winced inwardly. I extended my hand and asked him to come in, pardon the mess, and have a seat. He did. I closed the door behind him and took a seat myself.

Now I hope you don't think it impious or impudent. I didn't know what else to do, so I asked him what I could do for him. That's funny, when you stop to think about it: the Crucified, Risen and Ascended Lord, the Son of God, in my presence, and I presume to ask what I can do for him. I hope you appreciate the irony.

He didn't. He told me just exactly what I could do for him. He had just been released from prison in Massachusetts. He didn't tell me the crime and I didn't ask. Nor did he protest his innocence. His manner was very subdued as he told me his story.

He was on his way back home, which was somewhere in east Tennessee, to his wife and daughter whom he had seen only once in the past two years when they had managed to come north for a visit. He was anxious to get home, excited and a little apprehensive, knowing the job prospects for an ex-con weren't at all good and that his wife's salary could barely provide for mother and daughter, let alone a dependent husband.

"How are you traveling?" I asked.

"I've got an old pickup," he said. Then, after an awkward pause, but not defensively, he added, "It's mine. 'Was mine before I went in the joint and a buddy took care of it for me while I was in. It's a real gas and oil hog and I can't believe the way gas prices have gone up since I've been in. I've used up the money they gave me when I got released, and now I've got to get some gas to keep going. I'm running on fumes right now. I was hoping maybe you could help me out. You're the second reverend I've had to ask today."

There was that word again: sharp, cutting.

"I almost ran out just out of Harrisonburg and a reverend there helped me out."

"How long have you been traveling?" I asked.

"This is the third day. I'm pushing this old truck right hard. I just hope she gets me there."

"Where are you sleeping?"

"In the truck."

That, anyway, accounted for his unkempt appearance and his odor.

It was getting late. It was time for me to do something. His story wouldn't be too difficult to verify. Call the police for a check on the truck, possibly even call the prison in Massachusetts. It would all take time. Time I really didn't have just then.

I told him that I would have to do these things before I could help him.

He nodded, said he understood, and told me the name of the warden at the prison.

I told him the calls would not be necessary.

He nodded and smiled.

I told him that I couldn't give him cash, but that I would follow him to the 7-Eleven on Grandin Road. There we could fill his tank, get a quart of oil and something for him to eat. He had never mentioned food, but he must have been hungry.

"That'd be real nice," he said.

I arranged to get a check from the Pastors' Discretionary Fund, a fund that you, the members of Christ Lutheran Church, provide for just such occasions.

He pumped the gas while I went inside to get the oil, a sandwich and a pint of milk. I was anxious to get back to the office. I was still seeing this as an interruption — an unwelcome interruption, to be painfully honest; something keeping me from other things I should really be doing. I paid the bill, went outside, and gave him the oil and the food.

He said, "Thanks, I really appreciate it."

I was beginning to realize that this man was a little different from the dozens of other transients with whom I've come in contact. It was more what he didn't say than what he did say.

He never complained about how put upon he was. He never assured me that he was Born Again or even a "good Christian," and he never promised to pay the money back or offer to do some work to earn it, three things I have, I suppose, come to expect from those seeking help. He was, if you'll pardon a bad joke, a breath of fresh air in that respect.

He finished putting the oil in the truck, wiped his hands, stuck out the right one which I took and shook.

Then he did something very unsettling: As he shook my hand, he said, "Bless you, reverend."

Somehow I gathered the presence of mind to stammer, "And may God go with you, too."

Then he got in his truck, started it up, and pulled away. I returned to the church, but was unable to forget him or to feel completely satisfied with the financial Band-Aid we'd provided.

Some days later I started to prepare for this sermon and re-read the Gospel text appointed for the day:

> *"And Jesus took a child, and put him in the midst of them; and taking him in his arms, he said to them, 'Whoever receives one such child in my name receives me; and whoever receives me, receives not me but him who sent me.' "*

My study of the text revealed that far from being romanticized in those days, children — along with women and tax collectors — were considered, at best, second-class persons. Yet, Jesus says, whoever receives such a one receives me; indeed, receives God himself. It's not unlike that enigmatic passage in Matthew in which Jesus utters the mysterious sentence, "Inasmuch as you have done it to one of the least of these, my brothers, you have done it to me."

I devoutly believe that it is so. And therefore I decided to take the risk of making a fool out of myself this morning by telling you that Jesus Christ was in my office. Whether or not I "received him" I cannot tell and perhaps that is not for me to judge, anyway. But I do know that he was there even though I am not at all proud of the perfunctory manner in which I dealt with him.

Those of you who are experienced with people who ask for help may be saying to yourselves, "You know, there's a very good possibility you've been 'had': he could have been a clever and sincere-looking con artist."

Indeed he could have been. There's no denying that possibility. But isn't that the troublesome thing about dealing with this Jesus? He always leaves such decisions up to you, letting you risk being wrong, risk being made a sucker of, risk being had, risk betting your life and losing it. He is the One who asks, "Who do *you* say that I am?"

And I thank God that he is the same One who forgives wrong decisions, who loves and laughs with P. T. Barnum's suckers, who loves the gullible and the vulnerable in spite of themselves, who continues to come to us even when we fail to recognize let alone receive him, who continues to stand at the door and knock, who promises that those who bet their lives and lose them are precisely the ones who find life.

He is, by his own description, the little child, the second-class person, the outcast, the imprisoned, the stranger, the refugee, the depressed person, the alcoholic, the battered wife, the one who asks for gas to get home to his wife and daughter in east Tennessee.

Jesus Christ should not be so hard to identify — he has identified himself: "Whoever receives such a one receives me and him who sent me." He intrudes upon our affairs, interrupts our well-planned days. And we, therefore, can celebrate his presence among us, at least when we finally get past our busyness and preoccupation and realize that he is indeed among us.

Here is no demand. Here is gift and opportunity to receive our Lord and our God. The Church's oldest and most ardent prayer is "Maranatha — Come, Lord Jesus." It is a prayer he chooses to answer every day.

Meditation

Meditation, according to Webster's, is "solemn reflection on sacred matters as a devotional act." That struck me as a particularly appropriate discipline for Good Friday, and so I set out to enable those present at our Tenebrae Service to do just that.

I selected the St. Mark Passion and divided it into nine sections. Each meditation is a "solemn reflection" on one (and only one!) section of the narrative. I hoped to enable the worshipers to hear and take their place in each specific portion of the Passion narrative.

Apart from the style, the only device that runs throughout is the occasional use of theatre imagery ("denouement," "catastrophe," "scene for two," etc.), an intentional play on the term "the drama of redemption."

In the service, a section of the text was read, the appropriate meditation delivered, a good period of silence (one to two minutes) observed, a collect prayed and a candle extinguished. By the time the last two meditations were delivered, the worship room had been cast in total darkness.

Nine Meditations on the St. Mark Passion

I — THE PROPHECY

Text: *Mark 14:26-31*

Still they cannot understand
And still they cannot take him at his word.
He who rebuked the wind and said to the sea,
"Peace! Be still,"
Who cast out demons,
Healed the sick,
Cleansed lepers,
Fed thousands,
Made the deaf hear and the dumb speak;
He who even raised a little girl from death
Must still endure the folly of his followers.

When he told them to enter a town,
There to find a colt on which no one had ever sat,
Did they not find it so?
And when he told them as they went into the city
A man carrying a jar of water would meet and lead them
    to an upper room,
Did they not find it as he'd told them?
And still they cannot understand.
And still they cannot take him at his word.
"You will all fall away," he says.
But they say, "No! Not I!"
How can they see,

How understand,
That even while foretelling their defection,
Even while predicting their treason
Their master speaks to them a word of hope?
"After I am raised up," he says, "I will go before you.
Neither your faithless fleeing nor my impending death
Will sever our relationship.
The scattered flock will be gathered again
And I will be the Shepherd."

Bad news and worse predictions
Blind them, blind us,
To the underlying, over-arching goodness
Of the mystery we here celebrate, the drama we rehearse.
So still we cannot understand
And still we cannot take him at his word:
We will all indeed defect
And he must surely die.
But he is greater than our failure,
And will be death's undoing
And still will go before us
And still will be our Lord
And then
And only then
We'll understand
And take him at his word.

II — THE ANGUISH

Text: *Mark 14:32-42*

Contrast
Sharp, striking antitheses:
The Son of Man and the sons of men.
He: crushed by the sorrow in his heart,
Distress and bitter anguish
(Was it that he was not sure what this night held for him
Or rather that he knew too well
Or somehow both?):
"My soul is sick with sorrow,
A sickness unto death.
Stay here and watch."
They: stupified by wine and the lateness of the hour,
Ignorant of the drama playing 'round them and before
    them,
Unable to understand and unwilling to make the effort,
Sleep.
He: imploring his Father, Master of the Universe,
To spare him the hour of suffering;
Work unfinished,
Pain fierce,
Torment fearsome, cries
Take this cup away!
But if you will not — do not leave me in my hour
    of utmost need;
They: oblivious,
Fail him in this hour of need.
He: obedient to his Father's will
Obedient unto death
Even death on a cross;
They: disobedient to their Master's simple order,
Fail even to watch with him one hour.
He: opens his heart to suffering

And takes the path that leads thereto;
They: shield their hearts from suffering
And take their rest.
He accepts;
They do not even understand
And for that reason are his greatest cause of suffering.
The Son of Man deserted, disobeyed, betrayed
    into the hands of sinful men,
Now and forever. Amen

III — THE BETRAYAL

Text: *Mark 14:43-52*

Betrayal
Arrest
Seizure
Words from the world of politics
Competing views and ideologies
"We would change this, keep that."

Clubs
Swords
Capture
Words from the world of armies
Might makes right
Prevailing forces determine
What is changed, what kept.

They have in common power
The thirst for it
The struggle for it.
Jesus offends everybody, especially
Chief Priests
Scribes
Elders.

He would change what they would keep,
Keep what they would change.
What's more, he will not play the power game
Politically with power brokers
Militarily with Zealots
But claims authority of a different sort
And preaches
Love
Humility
Peace.

Clearly, any fool can see that he's
Too different
Too radical
Exceedingly naive;
And, with an ever-growing corps of followers,
A
Dangerous
Man.

Obviously, he must be stopped
On that all reasonable people surely can agree.
He is a threat to political stability,
Business as usual, the
Social
Economic
Religious
Status quo.

He must be stopped,
Dispatched
Once and for all.
But the betrayal must be handled with
Tact
Diplomacy
Finesse.

Embrace of a devotee
Kiss of a disciple
A bitter irony
The
Perfect
Touch

Chief priests
Scribes and
Elders were wrong,
And they were right:

Wrong in thinking they could by murder stop him
Or the God whose Kingdom he brought near;

But right, too:
He surely would change things;
Would even (God forbid) change us;
And that indeed makes him a
Very
Dangerous
Man.

HYMN: "Ah, Holy Jesus"

IV — THE DENIAL

Text: *Mark 14:53-72*

T. S. Eliot asks the awful question:
"Who shall stretch out his hand to the fire and deny his
    master?
And who shall be warm by the fire and deny his master?"

You are known by the company you keep
So choose your friends wisely and well.
My father taught me that.
Peter's father, too, quite likely taught his son the same.
We are all of us sufficiently guilty of real offenses;
Guilt by association is something none of us needs.

Good fathers also teach their sons to tell the truth.
One lie begets a dozen more.
A lie once told must be defended by further falsehoods.

Peter took a bit of comfort by the courtyard fire
Until a maid confronted him.
"You were with the Nazarene," she said.
And Peter's first untruth is told:
"I neither know nor understand your meaning."
The deed is done.
The lie is lied.
Guilt by association has been fended off.
Peter's claim's been staked
And now must be defended,
But only twice.
His third and most vigorous denial
Is the rooster's cue:
His raucous cry pierces the silence of the night
Pierces the heart of the lying disciple
And echoes in the abyss of his soul.

Break down and weep.
What else will silence that sound, this pain?

And in response to the direct question
"Are you the Christ, the Son of the Blessed?"
The master tells the simple truth
And gives the damning answer: I am indeed.
His Father taught him well.

And still, whenever I hear a rooster crow;
And still, when called to stake my claim,
Declare, defend my ultimate allegiance,
I shudder; sometimes, too,
Break down and weep
For once again, the poet's asked his awful question
And he's looking right at me.

V — THE CONDEMNATION

Text: *Mark 15:1-15*

What did I ever do to deserve the governorship
Of this godforsaken province
And these malcontented people?
Tedium relieved only by tension and contention;
Satisfy Rome: prevent insurrection; maintain order; remit
    taxes.
Satisfy the people: grant a prisoner clemency
    now and then.
Satisfy their clergy: let them think they've got some
    power;
Give them what they want within reason.
Juggle ideals and realities.
Make sacrifices — of principles and,
If need be,
Of people.

They drag that poor pathetic fool in here
After beating him to a pulp,
Face caked with blood and spit,
And they expect me to interrogate him
On trumped up charges of
Sedition, treason, insurrection, and
Plotting to overthrow the government.
First he refuses to give me a straight answer
And then he gives me none at all.
The chief priests are jealous,
The crowd riled up to passion pitch.
I try to steer a middle course.
(What idiocy — you can't reason with a mob.)
"WHAT DO YOU WANT ME TO DO WITH HIM?"

ALL RIGHT THEN,
FOR GOD'S SAKE
TAKE HIM OUT
AND CRUCIFY HIM!

For God's sake indeed.
And yours.
And mine.

VI — THE INSULT

Text: *Mark 15:16-20a*

Soldiers can be crude.
By means of a purple robe, a crown of thorns,
And counterfeit homage
They mock
Scorn
Ridicule
Humiliate
Deride
Satirize
Caricature
Degrade
Debase
Shame
And derogate.

What irony!
How could they know
The one who suffers their maltreatment
Reveals his royal dignity precisely in his silence
And so bears witness to God's saving plan
Fulfilled amid the very things
That seem to prove the opposite.
It is indeed a king they scorn,
And not just any king.
May God have mercy on their merciless souls,
And on ours, too.
For after all
Isn't that the point of this whole catastrophe?

HYMN: "O Sacred Head, Now Wounded"

VII — THE LONELINESS

Text: *Mark 15:20b-32*

Misery loves company.
I'll get by with a little help from my friends.
There's nothing that the two of us together can't handle.
Cliches
Bromides
Platitudes
And as with most such,
Not without an element of truth.

Physical anguish can be borne.
Ask those who have suffered debilitating diseases,
Extensive surgery
Extended convalescence.
Bearing up is difficult but not impossible.
The human animal is remarkably resilient.

Isolation is another matter.
To be outcast
Ostracized
Abandoned
Alone
Is a far more intense trial.

To have no one stand behind you or beside you;
To feel that no one gives a damn what happens to you;
To think that you could simply slip from the land of the
    living
And no tear would be shed
And no one would miss you
And some might even say "Thank God he's gone; good
    riddance;"
Humankind can't bear that sort of suffering long.

The soldiers have already had their sport with him
And now shoot craps to see who gets his clothes.
Chief priests and scribes now take their turn
At taunting and tormenting him.
Executions are entertainment to the passersby,
A morbid group of wags
Who hurl their blasphemies
Bereft of thought and comprehension.
Disciples, of course, are nowhere to be found.
The two stretched out across the black Judean skies
With him revile him, too,
And so deny him comradeship with those
    whose fate he shares.

And he, alone,
The Word of God incarnate,
Is without a word,
Without offense,
Without a friend.

It won't be too much longer now:
Humankind can't bear that sort of suffering long.

VIII — GODFORSAKEN

Text: *Mark 15:33-38*

The theatre goes dark
All other actors leave the stage
Or fade into the shadows.
This is a scene for two:
The Crucified and his Father.

Jesus spent his whole life
Proclaiming the nearness of God,
Revealing one who does not judge,
Bringing near to outcasts, sinners,
    the rejected and unclean
A God of grace who is not distant but at hand
To save and not to damn.

Jesus spent his whole life
In unmediated fellowship
With one whom he alone dared call "my Father;"
An intimacy unique, unparalleled:
The Father and his only Son.

Now, handed over to be crucified
As one accursed, rejected and despised,
A rebel to the Romans
And blasphemer to the Jews,
He suffers the ultimate torment that is hell:
The rejection and abandonment of the very one he called
    "my Father."

"My God, my God, why have you forsaken me?"
No seeming absence, misperception or mistake;
The real, profound abandonment of Jesus by his God.

This is no shout of confidence,
No victory cry; not this;
Instead a cry of utter dereliction.
And as his God forsakes him on the cross
He shouts the tortured question, "Why?"
No answer comes. And with a loud
    and deeply anguished cry
He dies defeated, rejected, desolate and broken.

This is a scene for two:
The Son of God and God the Father,
God against God
Not merely allowing this to happen
But himself active in the dying Christ.
A mystery profound as Jesus' suffering:
God suffers in and with the Son whom he forsakes
In order to reveal the boundless love of God for all.

This is a scene for two,
The crisis, the climax, the turning point.

Will the audience be moved?
Will the audience believe?

IX — THE CONFESSION

Text: *Mark 15:39-47*

"Truly this man was the Son of God."
A patent absurdity:
Profession of faith in the divine sonship
    of a dead derelict
By a pagan who supervised his execution
Motivated by the vision of his utter aloneness,
The sound of his expiring groan,
His weakness, helplessness and suffering;
Nonsensical by the reasoning of this world.
But that's God way
And that's God's Son now dead upon the tree.
Only in his suffering do we know him as God for us,
God with us in our suffering.
Bonhoeffer was right:
In this world, "only a suffering God can help."
And only such a God engenders trust and love.

The rest is denouement:
Claim his corpse and wrap it in a shroud,
And lay him in the tomb and roll the stone across.
Don't worry that you hadn't time to do
Too good a job.
He will not stay there long.

Montage

In his little book, Preaching Law and Gospel, my seminary preaching professor, dean and (later) president, Herman G. Stuempfle, Jr., describes what he calls "the montage form" as the "attempt to make some dimension of the Christian life real to our diverse listeners by flashing before them quick images of people who embody that dimension in actual life." Later, he calls such images "snapshots of reality."[1]

The greater part of the body of "Remember That You Are Dust" is such a montage. Taken as a whole, the sermon is really a hybrid, beginning with a narrative that establishes the refrain for the montage images which follow and concluding with a brief declarative section.

The Ash Wednesday liturgy uses a good deal of repetition: the imposition of ashes and individual absolution repeated for each worshiper; "the body of Christ, given for you; the blood of Christ, shed for you" said to each communicant; and, if used, the almost hypnotic repetitiveness of the Great Litany. The repetition of the phrase "Remember that you are dust" was a conscious attempt to blend the style of the sermon with the style of the liturgy.

[1]Herman G. Stuempfle, Jr., Preaching Law and Gospel (Philadelphia: Fortress, 1978), p. 71.

Remember That You Are Dust

Genesis 2:4b-7
2 Corinthians 5:20b—6:2

I have a vivid memory of an Ash Wednesday not too many years ago. The congregation went forward pew by pew to the chancel rail. Prayerful and penitent, we knelt to receive the absolution and the imposition of ashes.

First came the presiding minister. He laid his hands on the head of each person and said, "Receive the gracious forgiveness of all your sins in the name of the Father and of the Son and of the Holy Spirit." Each of us in turn responded, "Amen."

Behind the minister came the deacon, bearing a chalice of ashes, making a small cross on the forehead of each worshiper and whispering in his or her ear. He whispered in a voice so low that it was not until he came to me that I could hear what he was saying. As he traced the Cross of Christ on my forehead, he whispered, "Remember, man, that you are dust, and to dust you shall return."

Perhaps it was the intensity of the moment. Or perhaps it was the Spirit of God. But in either event, those sobering words seared their way indelibly into my mind.

In the days, weeks, and months that have followed, I have returned to those words many, many times.

They are, to me, a reminder of who I am. A member of the human race, the crown of God's glorious creation, yes. But at the same time, a creature molded out of the dust of the earth whose flesh is destined there to return.

In thinking about those words, in turning them over in my mind, I find that they say different things to me at different times. So what I'd like to do in the next few moments is simply to share with you some of the times when these words have rung particularly true and meaningful. If some of the examples sound like accusations, be assured that I stand indicted with you. If some of them hit pretty close to home, it's only because we share the common bond of broken humanity.

"Remember that you are dust." Sometimes these words serve as a pin to burst the balloon of arrogant pride.

When you begin to think that you are God's gift to your employer, remember that you are dust.

When you're convinced that a group or a committee cannot function properly in your absence, remember that you are dust.

When you have hurt someone, yet feel too proud to apologize, remember that you are dust.

Or when you have been wronged, yet refuse to accept a sincerely offered apology, remember that you are dust.

When you say to yourself, "If only more people would see things my way, we'd all be a lot better off," remember that you are dust.

When you've finally satisfied yourself that you really are better than the Joneses, remember that you are dust.

When you interrupt someone because what you have to say is obviously more important than what she has to say, remember that you are dust.

When you feel that God must hold you in higher esteem than others because you are, after all, a "pretty good person," remember that you are dust.

When you refuse an offer of help because you know right well that you can do a better job than he can, remember that you are dust.

When you feel that you are the genuine, archtypical self-made person, remember that it is God who has made us and not we ourselves, remember that you are dust.

"Remember that you are dust" — sometimes the words serve as a source of comfort, reminding us of our creatureliness, reminding us of our God-given limitations, reminding us that God is the Almighty, and we are not, reminding us that he made us a little *lower,* and not a little *higher,* than the angels.

So when you stick your foot in your mouth twice in the course of a three-minute conversation, remember that you are dust.

When something fails despite your best effort to make it succeed and you can't figure out why, remember that you are dust.

When you feel overwhelmed by the demands that are made of you and you wonder why you can't bear up under the strain, remember that you are dust.

When you feel angry, and then feel guilty for feeling angry, and then feel frustrated because you can't control your emotions, remember that you are dust.

When you suffer by comparison to anyone else, remember that you are *both* dust!

When you forget a good friend's name in the middle of an introduction, remember that you are dust.

When you are advised that unless you begin to take life easier, you're headed for a heart attack or stroke, remember that you are dust.

Yes, you are a child of God. Yes, you are loved and accepted as you are, but *no,* you are not without human limitations. Remember that you are dust.

Today, Ash Wednesday, we remember that we are indeed and in fact dust. We acknowledge our trespass, our weakness, our fault.

We confess that we are in need of rather large doses of grace, in need of humility, acceptance, forgiveness.

Yet at the same time, we also remember that our God is "gracious and merciful, slow to anger and abounding in steadfast love."

In Jesus of Nazareth, and particularly in his Passion and Death upon which we focus more intensely during this season of Lent, we see a God who withholds nothing from his children, but who loves and forgives freely and with no strings attached.

Today, even while acknowledging our unworthiness, even when clothed in ashes and dust, we receive a gift which, by our Lord's own design, is given for the forgiveness of sin. Not tomorrow when we have shaped up nor the day after when we have made amends; *now* we receive a foretaste of the feast to come.

Listen! Hear the word of God to you *today:*

"*Behold*, now *is the acceptable time;*
Behold, now *is the day of salvation.*"

This day; *these* times; now; you; accepted; loved; forgiven; freely.

There is nothing more to be said, save this alone:

"*Come, for all things are* now *prepared.*"

Vignette

This form is similar to the montage, but consists of somewhat longer, more complete units. In "Fragments," these units are all bits and snippets of conversations, but they could as easily be narratives, poems, questions. Each unit is intended to interpret one pericope from the appointed texts; the pericope therefore follows the vignette.

In working on this sermon, I encountered two problems. One had to do with the texts; the other with the form. The texts struck me as containing a good deal of law and not much gospel. I felt constrained to admit that at the very beginning of the sermon and to end it with the two vignettes that were good news, referring the listener to the Eucharist as the embodiment of that good news, the visible word of God's favor in spite of the brokenness depicted in the preceding vignettes.

The form itself tends to atomize the texts, uprooting them from their context, Sitz im Leben, canonical position and so forth. I intended to interpret the complete texts faithfully and let each pericope stand as a sort of "punch line" after its companion vignette. I'm not sure how successful I actually was, but I still believe the form has potential.

Fragments

1 Kings 19:14-21
Galatians 5:1, 13-25
Luke 9:51-62

All three of the texts appointed for today are rich in meaning and alive with possibility. They conjure up a whole host
of vignettes and fragments of conversations. So instead of
attempting to tie the three texts together in some contrived
and artificial way, my sermon this morning will simply be a
rather disjointed potpourri of these vignettes and fragments
of conversations, some imagined, some not.

As I worked with the texts, I became aware, as I am sure
you did as you heard them read, that they contain some very
hard — even harsh — sayings. I will not mitigate or com-
promise their hardness or their harshness, but only ask that
you trust that God, like all loving parents, must sometimes
say hard and harsh things to his balky and disobedient
children.

I

"Look, as a congregation we've already sponsored two
refugee families and we'll probably sponsor another. And
that's okay. But I have my doubts about going any farther
than that. You know how much time, energy, and money we've
already poured into refugee resettlement. I'm not so sure but
that it couldn't have been better spent elsewhere. I'm not sure
where, but, well, I don't know.

Other churches that concentrate more on getting new members or on doing TV shows are growing by leaps and bounds. We've grown some, I know, but not like them. I don't know. I just don't think we should spend so much time and energy on this refugee thing. There are other issues which demand our attention. I think we've already done our fair share."

No one who puts his hand to the plow and looks back is fit for the Kingdom of God.

II

"Honey, I look at it this way. We've been pretty liberal in our giving to the Church these past few years. I know we made the promise that we would increase our giving by 1 percent of our income per year and we've done that faithfully for three years and we're giving over $1,500 a year now. But when we made that promise, do you remember what the mortgage rate was? It was 7½ percent and $60,000 would buy the house of our dreams. If we're gonna buy any house like what you and I know we both want, then we're gonna have to make some cuts, and the way I see it, one of the things that's gonna have to be reduced is the amount we pledge. Maybe we can make it up later."

Foxes have holes and birds of the air have nests; but the Son of Man has nowhere to lay his head.

III

"I tell you, I don't know how many more meetings like that I can take. It's like butting heads constantly. Those people just don't seem to understand or even *care about* the mission of the Church. Oh, they'll talk endlessly about downspouting and paint and boilers and salaries. But do you think they see any connection whatsoever between their private little relationship with God and the nuclear arms buildup, the reduction of social services, the plight of the starving and homeless? Every meeting I raise the same issues and every meeting I get shouted down with some absurd platitude like, "What business is that of ours? That doesn't have anything to do with religion." They must think that they're supposed to run a club for spiritual types instead of overseeing the mission of the Body of Christ. They'll be relieved when my term is over, if they let me continue that long. I've heard talk they're going to suggest I resign. I know the pastor doesn't agree with them, but he's afraid of saying too much for fear of losing his job. He knows his predecessor got bounced out for being too involved in social ministry. And his wife has made it absolutely clear she likes this town and wants to stay a nice, long time; so he's not to make waves or create conflict.

God, I'm tired of this. Maybe I *ought* to resign and move my membership someplace else.

Elijah said to the Lord, "I have been very jealous for the Lord, the God of hosts: for the people have forsaken thy covenant, thrown down thine altars, and slain thy prophets with the sword; and I, even I only, am left; and they seek my life, to take it away."

IV

"This recession thing is driving me crazy. And it's playing havoc with my investments. I mean, it's not like I've got a lot of money tied up in it, but it's a lot to me, and I've gotta be careful with what happens to it.

I've thought about pulling my money out of the market, investing in a money market fund and then buying back in when the market bottoms out. But what if it starts to rise? I'll lose money. I could just sit tight and hope. Capital losses *are* tax deductible. I've even toyed with the idea of speculating a little. You know: commodities futures, short selling, that sort of thing. They say you can make a bundle when the market falls. But I don't know if that's for me.

The whole thing is so confusing it's got my stomach all tied up in knots and I just can't get it off my mind. I used to have a martini at lunch; now I drink Maalox. It's affecting my work at the office. I know my broker is getting sick of my questions; do you know I called him three times yesterday? My wife says the kids are forgetting what I look like; she says

58

my son had to draw a picture of his parents for school, and where my face should have been he drew a picture of the Wall Street Journal. Cute kid."

For freedom Christ has set us free; stand fast therefore, and do not submit again to a yoke of slavery.

V

"Look, I know what you're asking me to do is important. And I believe in it; I really do. I think that we as Christians need to be involved in this sort of thing, and I'm honored that you would ask me to be one of the leaders. But I'm afraid that now just isn't the right time for me. I'm under an incredible amount of pressure at work. And quite frankly, I've taken on too much responsibility at the lodge. I intend to back off of some of that after my term is up, but that's not until after the first of the year. And, you know, my family isn't exactly supportive of my involvement in the church. I think you can count on me to help, but not until I get rid of some of these other obligations."

Leave the dead to bury their own dead; but as for you, go and proclaim the Kingdom of God.

VI

"I'm not sure I understand. You're saying a person is saved by God for Christ's sake and that that person contributes nothing on his or her part?"

"That's what I'm saying. It's an either/or situation: either trust God or trust yourself, but not a combination."

"And you're saying that spreading the gospel means telling just that to other people and trusting God to create faith by means of the telling?

"Right again, Boy Wonder. As Saint Paul says, 'Faith comes through hearing.' "

"All right. But if my works have nothing to do with my salvation, if Christ has freed me from — as you put it — the demands of the law, then what's to stop me from living as I darned well please?"

"How do you mean?"

"Oh, I mean, just for the sake of argument now, doing drugs, sleeping around, gratifying the senses, that sort of thing."

"Is that what you really want?"

"I think about it sometimes. I think it might be fun."

"Might be. Probably safe to say that it would be fun. But you didn't answer the question: Is that what you really want?"

"No, that's the strange thing: I really can't say that it is. I'm not put together that way. But I still think about it."

You were called to freedom, brethren, only do not use your freedom as an opportunity for the flesh. Those who belong to Christ Jesus have crucified the flesh with its passions and desires

VII

"I just can't seem to sense the presence of God in my life. God knows, I want it. I trust him. I know he loves me. But he is so silent. His absence is more common than his presence. He seems so exacting, so demanding at times, but I don't know what he expects of me. And his absence and his silence frighten me, confuse me, confound me, and anger me. How can I know this loving and demanding God? And how can I know that he cares one whit about me and about this world I live in?"

The body of Christ given for you. The blood of Christ shed for you.

Fill the moments with silence and reflect.

Parable

It is unassailable dogma among scholars that parables make one point, reach a single conclusion, while allegories are of the A is really Z, B equals Y, C corresponds to X and so on variety. And the issue is complicated when we realize (and attempt to explain to parishioners) that some of Jesus' parables have suffered allegorization at the hands of later compilers and editors.

In Telling the Story, Richard A. Jensen is candid about the difficulty of sticking to one point: "If you have not tried it before (creating parables), you will find, I think, that your first efforts . . . are by nature allegorical."[1]

"The Alchemist" is an attempt at using a parable to make the one main point I hear St. Paul making in his letter to the Galatians. I did first tell the congregation that the morning's sermon would be in the form of a parable and invited them to imagine along with me. Departing from the traditional sermonic style and form, I hoped such advance notice would help to include them rather than shock and alienate them. I then re-read the text and told the parable.

[1] Richard A. Jensen, Telling the Story Minneapolis: Augsburg, 1980), p. 154.

The Alchemist

Galatians 1:6-7; 3:1-5; 5:7

Hilary was an alchemist, of sorts. He had apprenticed no small number of years with the old master, Bartholomew. It was not widely known; indeed, it was an extremely well-kept secret that old Bartholomew had actually attained the elusive goal of alchemy: he had succeeded in transmuting lead into gold.

Countless hundreds of his predecessors and contemporaries had striven long and hard to do what Bartholomew had done quite by accident. One particularly unproductive afternoon, Bartholomew decided to call it a day. He straightened up his workroom and put his tools and materials away. "A place for everything and everything in its place" his mother had taught him while he was still a lad, and that had become the unwritten law of his laboratory.

He hung up his apron and took one last look around the room to make sure he had extinguished all the candles. No sooner had he opened the door that led from his workroom into his living quarters than his cat came bounding into the workshop with his dog in close pursuit.

Amid barks and growls and hisses and Bartholomew's vain efforts to get the beasts out of the lab, tubes and vials and beakers shattered to the floor, elaborate equipment was toppled over; and chemicals of all sorts formed pools and rivulets which ran and dripped every which way.

When the cat ran between his legs with the dog hot on her heels, no longer chasing, but simply attempting to escape the chaos, even old Bartholomew wound up in a heap on the floor.

From that unlikely and undignified vantage point, he saw it: In the middle of that dreadful mess lay a bar of what had, moments ago, been lead, no longer dull and grey, but glimmering and glittering the unmistakable rich, deep amber of gold. At first Bartholomew thought it to be coated with sulphur that had spilled and mixed with some liquids. But upon closer examination, he found that it was indeed pure and solid gold, 24-karat through and through.

At first he was puzzled; then he was frustrated as he realized that there was no way he could ever figure out what had happened. Then he just threw back his head and laughed at the absurdity of the whole affair.

In succeeding weeks, Bartholomew found that if he re-created the accident, sometimes the lead would change into gold, and sometimes it wouldn't.

At first this perturbed him, but after a while he contented himself that sometimes would just have to be enough.

As Bartholomew grew older, he realized his obligation to pass on his knowledge (if indeed it could be called knowledge) and so Hilary became his apprentice. Hilary learned how to set up the accident and how to get a dog and a cat to cooperate and together he and Bartholomew made gold out of lead, at least some of the time.

After Bartholomew died, Hilary began to have doubts about what he was doing. "If a thing works," he thought, " then a good alchemist should understand *why* it works. Repeating an experiment with consistent and predictable results is one of the cornerstones of scientific method."

And so he set himself to the task of figuring out why sometimes the lead became gold. Every day he became more and more meticulous and precise and every day he became proportionately frustrated and confused.

One day a new thought occurred to him: "Perhaps if I can turn the gold back into lead, then I can determine why it sometimes works the other way."

In the days that followed, Hilary found it surprisingly easy to turn gold into lead. And he understood precisely why it worked. But still he could not turn the lead into gold. He could only re-create the accident and be content that sometimes it worked and sometimes it didn't. But content with this he was determined not to be. Indeed, the uncertainty of the whole thing became an unbearable conundum for him. And so he resolved, out of respect for his own integrity as an alchemist and in order to avoid further frustration, that he would no longer recreate the accident.

For the remainder of his days, Hilary devoted himself carefully and meticulously and predictably to turning Bartholomew's gold back into lead.

Allegory

"Wet Dog: A Christmas Story" was written for an early Christmas Eve service to which families with younger children traditionally come. For children, the story (which actually happened) provided an opportunity to tell the Christmas story in highly unspiritual, earthy terms and to do so with a little humor. For adults, it was another opportunity to "overhear" the gospel.

I didn't explain the allegorical elements. To say, "The dog's predicament is symbolic of our caughtness; the rope, the power of sin and the law; the yard, the world we live in" and so on, would be over the children's heads and unnecessary (I hope!) for the adults and in both cases terribly flat-footed and heavy-handed. Making an explicit connection with God's action in the Nativity, however, seemed quite necessary, particularly for younger hearers and marginally churched adults.

Wet Dog: A Christmas Story

Luke 2:1-20

Have you ever noticed how much storytelling goes on at Christmastime?

In our home, our 3-year-old daughter Jessica has been telling the same story for weeks now. Her story is, "I've been a good girl this year." That's her story, or more accurately, her *side* of the story.

In some homes, it's a tradition that a classic story such as Charles Dickens' "A Christmas Carol" or Dylan Thomas' "A Child's Christmas in Wales" or the old stand-by "'Twas the Night Before Christmas" be read or recited on Christmas Eve. That's a different sort of storytelling.

But most of the storytelling we do is simply sharing with others the events and happenings in our lives: remembrances of Christmases past, stories about shopping or finding a gift or finding a parking space at Tanglewood Mall. Listen these next few days and I think you'll be surprised at how much of our conversation can appropriately be described as "storytelling."

This strikes me as especially appropriate at this time of year. Because you and I and millions of others gather around and celebrate tonight and this Season The Story — God's Story. The Story of his coming among us as one of us. The story of the birth of Jesus, God's Son and our Savior.

So this evening, I'll tell a story. It's a story about one of the members of my family. Some of you know that just about a year ago now, the Radeckes acquired a very small black puppy. His name is Digby and I'd like to introduce him to you.

Digby is black. All black. All black from the tip of his very wet nose to the tip of his constantly churning whip of a tail. His mother was an Irish Setter and his father ... well, nobody but his mother knows who his father is, but he must have looked something like King Kong. When we first acquired him, we were told his father was probably a black Labrador Retriever. But as Digby has grown — and grown, and grown — he has begun to look quite like a Great Dane. He is now sufficiently tall enough to put his front paws on my shoulders, and the vet says he's not finished growing yet.

Now those of you who are familiar with the story of Winnie the Pooh know that Pooh was a bear of Very Little Brain. Digby is Pooh's Intellectual Equal. He buries bones and forgets where he's buried them. Last summer he buried an ice cube and was greatly perplexed when he tried to dig it up again. If you throw a ball or a stick to the left, he's likely to run to the right. He is clumsy and awkward, a very messy eater and drinker, and earnestly believes that the family room sofa is his own possession.

Digby has one saving grace. He is sweet and kind and gentle to a fault. He only barks at the letter carrier when she forgets or neglects to pet and play with him. The same is true of prowlers and burglars.

Digby is so big that he is able to get over our backyard fence. Notice I didn't say "jump the fence." He's not that graceful. Instead, he sort of mashes the fence down in one place and ambles over it.

Because he is able to do this and because he is too dumb to be afraid of the Grandin Road traffic, we have to keep him tied to our back porch when he is outside. His rope is quite long, and it is the rope and the problems Digby manages to get into because of that rope that concern us this evening.

About a week and a half ago, Digby was tied up outside. It was a particularly cold and rainy night, but he wanted to go out and, or course, when a dog wants out, out he goes.

About three minutes later, he began to whimper and whine. For Digby that usually means only one thing: he has managed to get his rope wrapped around and tangled up in something so that he's unable to get back on the porch.

So I looked out the window and sure enough, he had gone *under* the picnic table, *around* a large mock orange bush and was now quite stuck *atop* the picnic table, unable to move more than two or three feet.

I put on my slippers and went out onto the porch. He wasn't terribly tangled up at this point. If he would only retrace his steps, get down off the table, go around the bush and back under the table, he'd be free.

Like a fool, I tried to explain this to him. "Get down off the table, Digby." He thought I was yelling at him, so he tucked his tail between his legs and drooped his floppy black ears and looked guilty.

Then, I tried gestures. Go *down* and *around* and back *under*. Of course, he didn't understand.

Then I had a brilliant idea. I picked up a bone from the porch and threw it to the left. He tried to go to the right.

Next I tried pulling on the rope, thinking he'd back up. But the harder I pulled, the more he strained to come forward and, naturally, to get unstuck, he had first to go backward.

By now it was clear I would not be able to free him without descending from the porch and going to him. This I did. I figured he'd follow if I led the way, so I got down off the porch and tried to lead him out of his predicament. I did succeed in leading him off the table, at which point he managed to get the now-loose rope wrapped around his neck and right hind leg. Every time he tried to take a step, he choked himself.

I did the only thing there was left to do: I cut the rope, picked Digby up, and brought him back in the house. Both of us were cold and wet and shivering and both of us smelled like wet dog. But he was free and we were both back inside.

End of story.

Now that may not sound much like a Christmas story, but I assure you that that is indeed what it is and not just because it happened at Christmastime.

When God decided the time was right to set us free and show the depth of his love for us, he didn't holler at us or gesture to us or toss us a bone or pull on our rope or even simply show us the way by leading us.

When God decided to free us and show us his love, he came down to where you and I are. He cut the rope we're all tied up in, picked us up, and carried us back to himself.

But there's one important difference between the way I freed Digby and the way God frees us. God actually became one of us. He was born a helpless baby just as you and I were. He lived among us that we might come to know him and he died for us that we might come to love him, even as he already loved us.

And that is the Story we celebrate tonight. God's birth — his coming to us on a cold, dark, rainy night to set us free and bring us to himself.

That's why we're here. That's why we're happy. And that's why I wish you a most blessed and merry Christmas. For the God who came to us that first Christmas comes to you and sets you free this Christmas.

To *you* this night is born a child.

Visual Aid

"Go Fly a Kite" was a children's sermon that grew into the sermon for the day. It's a type of allegory that uses the parts of a standard, diamond-shaped kite as its visual referent, displayed in the front of the worship room.

Visual aids are powerful mnemonic devices and yet I, as much as or more than most preachers, shy away from them, except for children's sermons where their use is almost universally expected. I vigorously affirm that the preacher's task is to proclaim the living Word and that "faith comes through hearing." I feel we need to help our people use their ears to imagine and be drawn into community. Visual symbols can tend to be too rationalistic and isolating. But, carefully and sparingly employed, they can also become vehicles for proclaiming the good news.

Go Fly a Kite

Philippians 3:4-9

Introduction

It's March and we're in the middle of a season called Lent — a time for thinking about the meaning of Jesus' suffering and death and what it means to us who call ourselves his followers, who call ourselves by his name.

It's also kite-flying time. I enjoy kite-flying and have lost more than a few kites to trees, high winds, electrical and telephone wires, and kamikaze dives.

It seems to me that some people think that their relationship with God is just like flying a kite. So I thought I'd use my kite as an illustration of what I mean.

I

Now it's true that to get a kite to fly, the tail has to be just so — straight, not too short, not too long — providing just the right balance to prevent spins and nose-dives.

Some people think that's how it is with God's love. In order to get God to like them and to love them, they feel that they have to — you should pardon the expression — keep their tails in line. Be just so. Behave ever so properly.

They're afraid if things aren't just quite right, if they make a mistake or do something wrong, that God will not love them, that — like the kite with a too-short tail — they'll be thrown to the ground broken and smashed.

Martin Luther was one person who felt that way when he was young. He was convinced that God did not love him. So he set out on a journey to do all the right things that people believed would make God love them. He joined a monastery, prayed constantly, ate and drank very little; he even beat himself with a whip to punish himself for such little mistakes as singing the wrong note in the worship service. And even after all that, he still didn't feel that God loved him.

Then all of a sudden it dawned on him that God doesn't love his children *only* when they do right, when they keep their tails in line; he loves them all the time, "for the sake of his dear Son, Jesus Christ, our Lord." Even when he is displeased with our behavior, like parents who are displeased with their children's behavior, he doesn't stop loving us. You've probably heard it said before that God hates the sin but loves the sinner. Well, that is certainly so. His love for us does not depend upon our keeping our tails just so. God loves us freely in spite of what we do, so let's just take that tail off the kite.

II

It's also true that to get a kite to fly, you've got to have some string — a harness and a lead line. Any experienced and seasoned kite flyer can tell you that the art of kite flying lies almost entirely in how you maneuver the string. Pull it in when it's flying too low, let it out when a breeze takes it up. Pull on it to get it to climb. Do loops and dives and all sorts of tricks.

Some people think that's how it is with God's love. They can accept that God loves us even when our behavior isn't what it ought to be. But they still feel that there are some strings attached to that love. For instance — God will only love us if we love him in return. Or God will only love us if we read the Bible or go to church or go to Sunday School or be kind to small animals, or respect our parents, and so on and on.

They believe that there are just certain minimal conditions God sets up. Make no mistake — I believe God does indeed want us to do all these things — love him in return, read the Bible, pray to him, worship him, learn about him, treat his other creatures kindly, and honor and respect those in authority.

He expects that of us. But what he does not do is make those things the condition of his loving us. If we fail to do all of those things — God will surely be disappointed in us and saddened by our selfish behavior. But he will not stop loving us.

I know that's hard to understand and accept. Human beings don't love that way, at least not for very long. But God does — it's called "unconditional love" — no conditions, no ifs, ands, or buts. Or to use our example: God's love is a love that has no strings attached. So let's get rid of those strings.

III

It is also true that to get a kite to fly, you've got to have a covering of some sort. Coverings can be very elaborate: like this silk bird kite some friends gave me a few years ago, and which I will never even attempt to fly. Or the covering can be very ordinary or homemade — kites made out of the Sunday funny papers. You certainly won't get a kite up into the air without a covering.

Some people think that's how it is with God's love. They think that the covering is very important to God. There are lots of coverings:

What church we belong to, what kind of reputation we have, what school we go to, how pleasant and cooperative we are, where we work and what we do for a living, what kind of grades we get, what clubs we belong to, what teams we play on and how often we win, and how much money we make, where we live, what we think about certain things.

But God does not base his love upon our reputation or social position or rank or whether other people think we're popular or not. Jesus was forever getting into trouble because he sat down and ate with all the people whom the respectable religious folks of his day thought were dirty and to be avoided.

He didn't care about coverings. He just loved. And we say that Jesus is God. So if Jesus loved people without worrying about their coverings, that means that God loves people without worrying about their coverings. So let's just get rid of this cover.

IV

In kite flying, it's really important to have a good frame. If there's no frame, no structure, then no matter how precise the tail is, how flashy your work with the string, how fancy the covering, the thing just won't get off the ground. Or, if the frame breaks in the air, the kite will come fluttering ungracefully and unceremoniously earthward, and land in a pathetic heap.

This is where we find, at last, a similarity between kite-flying and God's loving us and the season of Lent. As Christians, we believe the sign of how much God loves us is the Cross of Jesus Christ. God could simply have judged us and rejected us since our tails are always out of line, our coverings are inadequate and we fail to pull the strings in just the right way.

But he didn't do that. Instead, he took all our shortcomings, all our rejection of him, all our disobedience and lack of trust, and he took that all upon himself in the person of Jesus. It is precisely because of Christ's death on the Cross that we know God loves us not through anything we do, but through everything he has done. This is all that counts: the Cross of Christ.

I know that's not easy to believe, just as this cross is not easy to see from the back of the church. But even when we lose sight of the Cross, it is still there. It's the basis and the center of our relationship with God. He loves us and we see the height and the depth of that love when we look upon the Cross.

V

There's one thing more — the bowstring. And that is just a reminder during this season of Lent that God bends over backwards to make his love a living reality in our lives.

It is this love and this bending over backwards that I would have you consider in the coming weeks, and in the silence of the next few moments.

Extended Illustration

It seems to me that much propositional preaching could be rescued from its prosaic captivity if only it had a concrete point of reference to which all the listeners could refer. An extended illustration can provide just such a referent.

By extended illustration, I mean a single narrative of greater length than the usual sermonic anecdote presented once and recalled a number of times in order to bring the propositions of the sermon down to cases, to illumine the propositions. The extended illustration could come from the world of literature, drama, hymnody, the daily newspaper or any number of other sources.

In "Equus and Worship," scene twenty-five from Peter Shaffer's brilliant play is introduced and performed. The sermon follows immediately thereafter so that the scene and the sermon form a single unit.

INTRODUCTION

In 1975 the Tony Award for Best Play was awarded to Peter Shaffer for his powerful and provocative play EQUUS. The play concerns Alan Strang, a disturbed seventeen-year-old boy who has created his own private religion — a religion in which he worships horses; hence the play's title: "equus" is the Latin word for "horse."

Alan worships his gods in intense and elaborate rituals. One evening in a fit of terror, guilt, and rage he systematically blinds six thoroughbreds with a steel spike and is committed to a psychiatric hospital.

At the hospital Martin Dysart is his psychiatrist, and while treating Alan he becomes painfully aware of the radical difference between Alan's passionate spirit and his own timid, dilute, civilized spirit.

In our scene, Dysart converses with Hester Salomon, the magistrate who committed Alan and a personal friend of Dysart. As the scene opens, Dysart has just left Alan who has talked about "truth drugs."

Equus and Worship

Matthew 4:8-10

"Without worship you shrink, it's as brutal as that . . . I shrank my own life. No one can do it for you. I settled for being pallid and provincial, out of my own eternal timidity."

The painful awareness of Martin Dysart: In the place of any living, vibrant worship, he has only a facsimile, an imitation as fake as his reproduction statue of Dionysus. He sees the vitality of Alan Strang's worship and, though he knows it to be distorted and tortured, he covets it: "That boy has known a passion more ferocious than I have felt in any second of my life. And let me tell you something: I envy it." He feels accused because of his sham devotion; Alan's stare says to him, "At least I galloped! When did you?"

There are at least two essential differences between Alan's worship and that of Martin Dysart and they can help us as we think about our worship as a Christian community. The first has to do with the object of worship and the second, the vitality of worship.

It is clear that Alan believes his god is a living god, Equus, the spirit he feels resides in all horses. By contrast, Dysart's devotion belongs to an idea, a notion, a bygone era, symbolized by books that can be put away, to be brought out only when desired, and a statue — an idol, if you will — that sits predictably and undemandingly on the mantle.

The object of Alan's worship is another being. The object of Dysart's in the last analysis is himself. Alan wholeheartedly gives himself in worship to another; Dysart is confined cautiously to himself, held back by his own "eternal timidity."

These factors, of course, influence the vitality of their worship. For Alan it is, "with my body, I thee worship!" For Dysart, fireside reading and a yearly pilgrimage with all the comforts of home.

What shall we say to these things? That our worship as a Christian community is more often like that of the timid and cautious Dysart than the adoring and passionate Alan? There is some truth to that.

That the object of our worship is too often our new likes and dislikes — too high church, too low church; too much new stuff, too much old stuff; too many German hymns, not enough German hymns? There's some truth in that, too.

That we are sometimes overly preoccupied with the "what" of worship and not concerned enough about the "who" we are worshiping? Also true.

That we are perhaps a bit too sophisticated for our own good at times? Again, true. Annie Dillard, one time Roanoker and Pulitzer Prize winner, has said, "The higher Christian churches — where, if anywhere, I belong — come at God with an unwarranted air of professionalism, with authority and pomp, as though they knew what they were doing, as though people in themselves were an appropriate set of creatures to have dealings with God . . . In the high churches they saunter through the liturgy like Mohawks along a strand of scaffolding who have long since forgotten their danger."[1]

Does this all mean that we ought to throw out the liturgy and throw up our hands with spontaneous and emotion-filled shouts of "Praise the Lord!" and "Hallelujah!"? It might do us good to do that once in a while. But a steady diet of it can get to be just as self-centered and subjective as Dysart's devotion. The content of worship comes to be unrestrained emotionalism. The context is simply the here and now. And the chief object to get the adrenaline running.

Liturgical worship can help us to forget ourselves and focus instead on the one we're worshiping, with integrity and in continuity with worshiping communities of the past as well as the present. There is truth in all these things.

---

[1] *Holy the Firm*, Harper and Row, New York, 1977, p. 59.

But there is one crucial difference that sets our worship apart from that of *both* Alan Strang and Martin Dysart.

Both of these characters have chosen their own gods and created their own *private* religion, while our confession is that God has chosen us and created the *community* that worships him. As Luther put it in his explanation to the Third Article of the Apostles' Creed, "I believe that I cannot by my own understanding or effort believe in Jesus Christ my Lord, or come to him. But the Holy Spirit has called me through the Gospel, enlightened me with his gifts and sanctified and kept me in true faith. In the same way he calls, gathers, enlightens and sanctifies the whole Christian Church on earth . . . "

In this worshiping community, we not only address God with prayer, praise, and thanksgiving; he addresses us, another difference.

He speaks his Word to us in the absolution. He grabs us by our ears and says, "You! For Christ's sake, I forgive you your sins and accept you as pure and holy."

He speaks to us in the reading and proclaiming of his Word, for properly understood, these are not merely words about God, they are the Word of God; they are not merely words *about* grace and faith and forgiveness, they are words that actually *give* God's grace which creates faith and declares us forgiven; words which actually do what they say they will do — nothing less than bring about a new creation. "Listen," God says, "you are mine — that is my decision and my completely unconditional gift to you."

He speaks to us in his visible, tangible and "tasteable" words, the Sacraments; for properly understood, they are not mere rituals or commemorations. They are the visible words of God, which do what they say they will do. "I baptize you. I wash you clean. I drown the old Adam in you and raise you up a new creation."

"This is the Body of Christ. It is given for you to forgive sins. Take it and eat it. This is the Blood of Christ shed for you to make a new covenant. Take it and drink it."

He speaks to us in his Word incarnate and reveals himself to be the God who is totally and unreservedly *for us*. He humbles himself and becomes obedient unto death, even death on a cross.

Or, to borrow Martin Dysart's language, "He has known a passion more ferocious than I have felt in any second of my life." And he had done it all *for us.*

Our worship, then, is a hearing of this Word of the living God, and a grateful response to it and to him.

There is something entirely appropriate about a dramatist concerning himself with the art of worship, for it is no exaggeration to call the liturgy a drama. Søren Kierkegaard offers an intriguing perspective on the intimate relationship between worship and theatre in his book, "Purity of Heart is to Will One Thing." In the theatre, he says, one will find a prompter, an actor, and an audience. Too often in worship, we think of God as the prompter, the minister as the actor, and the congregation as the audience. But so to understand worship is to render it empty and meaningless. Kierkegaard suggests that we think instead of the minister as prompter, every worshiper as an actor, and God as the "critical theatregoer, who looks on to see how the lines are spoken and how they are listened to." Such an understanding reminds us that our concern is not so much whether the "script" and the "performance" are pleasing and meaningful *to us,* the actors, but whether they are at all pleasing *to God,* the audience and object of our drama or worship. To God *alone* be glory.

Because God's Word is a word that forgives and sets free, we as actors in this drama of worship need not be restricted any longer by our own "eternal timidity." We can risk liturgical failure and missed notes. And more importantly, we can risk putting our whole being into our worship — to glorify God with all our heart, soul, mind, and strength; to rival the angelic chorus with our robust rendition of the Sanctus; to forget our own querulousness and become "lost in wonder, love and praise," as one hymn puts it, knowing that the ones who lose themselves are precisely the ones who God promises will find themselves.

"Without worship you shrink, it's as brutal as that." Thanks be to Christ, for he is worthy of worship.

Chancel Drama

I have a pet theory to explain the proliferation of low-quality chancel dramas. It goes like this: One fine day, Pastor Hans Wurst decides that three weeks hence, his sermon will be in the form of a chancel drama. He checks the appointed Scripture texts for the day and finds the Parable of the Good Samaritan. Diligent pastor that he is, he sets out to read every existing chancel drama on that parable. He finds that there are one hundred of them. After reading all one hundred, he rightly concludes that all one hundred are terrible. Thereupon, he writes the one hundred and first. And so it goes.

Although I firmly believe that playwriting is best left to playwrights, I took a chance one Lent and wrote the one hundred and first chancel drama — a chancel comedy, to be more precise — on the Parable of the Prodigal Son. I did so for a rather simple reason. As I dealt with the text, I felt one overwhelming need as a preacher: to get out of the way of the explosive power of this magnificent story. I hoped this simple drama might allow me to do that. I wanted the congregation to experience the parable's event of grace: the Father's astonishing embrace of his wayward son. Set in relief against what the Father's response might have been, that embrace has tremendous impact.

Permission is hereby granted to perform the chancel drama without royalty. Due credit should be given as follows: "Written by Mark Wm. Radecke. Produced by permission of C.S.S. Publishing Company."

The Return of the Prodigal: The Way It Wasn't

Luke 15:11-32

Our Lord told the story we call "the parable of the prodigal son" much as you or I would tell a joke. He sets the situation up carefully and then hits us with the punchline: the father's unbelievable response to his wayward son's return. The problem is: we've already heard that one. So we don't laugh. To make matters worse, we've heard it so many times (in church, of course, where laughter is one form of music too rarely played) that we don't even realize it *is* a joke. Only when we grasp the absurdity of the father's response do we begin to understand that this is no mere earthly father. And then we can appreciate why Jesus told this heavenly, high and holy joke in the first place.

The father could have (we might even say he *should* have) reacted differently to his son's return. What if he had? . . .

Director: O.K. I'm having a little trouble with this scene. In scene 1, you remember, the son tells his father to give him his share of the inheritance, which the father does. It's sort of like the son telling his dad to "drop dead."

In Scene 2, the son goes off, has a fantastic time in the big city, and blows the whole wad partying. When a famine comes along, he winds up slopping hogs. When the slops start to look real good to him, he decides it's time to go home. At least there he can get three hots and a cot as a hired hand.

So in Scene 3 he sets out on the return trip. Along the way

he rehearses the speech he hopes will soften the old man's heart so that at least he won't slam the door in his face: "Father, I have sinned against heaven and against you. I am no longer worthy to be called your son."[1]

The problem is the father's response. I can't find a motivation for it. It doesn't make sense, so I want you to explore some other possibilities. *(Hands Father a list.)*

Father: You mean play out the scene of the son's return, but show you some different responses. Right?

Director: That's it.

Father: Fine. I was having some trouble with that line the way it's written, anyhow.

Director: Okay. We'll be shooting these to see how they look on film. Places, please.

Assistant: The Return of the Prodigal: Act 1, Scene 4, Take 1.

Son: *(enters, kneels)* Father, I have sinned against heaven and against you. I am no longer worthy to be called your son.

Father: Well, you got that right, boy!

Director: Cut. Try it again.

Assistant: The Return of the Prodigal: Act 1, Scene 4, Take 2.

Son: *(enters, kneels)* Father, I have sinned against heaven and against you. I am no longer worthy to be called your son.

Father: Let me see if I got this right. After what you've done, you want me to take you back. *(Son nods. Father finds this highly amusing)* That's a good one.

---

[1] From *Telling the Truth* by Frederick Buechner; Harper & Row, p. 67.

Director: Cut.

Assistant: The Return of the Prodical: Act 1, Scene 4, Take 3.

Son: *(enters, kneels)* Father, I have sinned against heaven and against you. I am no longer worthy to be called your son.

Father: Well, I hope you've learned your lesson. Are you ready to settle down now?

Director: Cut.

Assistant: The Return of the Prodigal: Act 1, Scene 4, Take 4.

Son: *(enters, kneels)* Father, I have sinned against heaven and against you. I am no longer worthy to be called your son.

Father: I certainly hope you can find some way to make this up to your mother, young man.

Director: Cut.

Assistant: The Return of the Prodigal: Act 1, Scene 4, Take 5.

Son: *(enters, kneels)* Father, I have sinned against heaven and against you. I am no longer worthy to be called your son.

Father: Hey, it's ok! Every red-blooded boy's gotta sow a few wild oats. Why, when I was your age . . .

Director: Cut.

Assistant: The Return of the Prodigal: Act 1, Scene 4, Take 6.

Son: *(enters, kneels)* Father, I have sinned against heaven and against you. I am no longer worthy to be called your son.

Father: Well, your mother and I have discussed the possibility that you might return. Now we don't think it would be fair to your older brother if we just took you back in. So we've proposed a program we're calling "earned re-entry."

Assistant: The Return of the Prodigal: Act 1, Scene 4, Take 7.

Son: *(enters, kneels)* Father, I have sinned against heaven and against you. I am no longer worthy to be called your son.

Father: You wanna know what suffering is? Just wait till you've got children of your own!

Director: Cut.

Assistant: The Return of the Prodigal: Act 1, Scene 4, Take 8.

Son: *(enters, kneels)* Father, I have sinned against heaven and against you. I am no longer worthy to be called your son.

Father: What I hear you saying is "I don't feel real good about myself." Can you tell me some more about that?

Director: Cut. *(approaches actors)* Those responses all make sense. But somehow I get the feeling we're missing something.

Father: Maybe we've got this thing all turned around.

Director: What do you mean?

Father: Well, suppose the point is precisely that the father's response *is* unbelievable. That it's supposed to be unbelievable. That the Father doesn't do what any other father on earth would do because he *isn't* an earthly father.

Director: A heavenly father, then?

Father: Right.

Director: Oh, good grief. God doesn't act like that. Where's the justice? Where's the anger?

Father: What makes him angry is his children refusing to believe he can be so loving, so merciful.

Director: As merciful and loving as a father who takes his prodigal son back with open arms, no questions asked?

Father: And throws a party to boot.

Director: If that's the way it is, this shouldn't be called the Parable of the Prodigal *Son.* It's the father who's the prodigal: lavish, almost excessive with his love.

Father: Like I said, unbelievable. And that's the point. The son can't believe it; he can't control it. He can only accept it and be grateful for it.

Director: All right. Let's try it the way it's written.

Assistant: The Return of the Prodigal: Act 1, Scene 4, Take 9

Son: *(begins to enter and kneel)* Father . . .

Father: *(runs to him, hugs him, holds a long moment)*

Son: Father, I have sinned against heaven and against . . .

Father: *(not hearing; to servants off)* Quickly! Bring the best robe, and put it on him; and put a ring on his hand, and shoes on his feet; and let us eat and make merry: *(to son)* for this, my son was dead, and is alive again; he was lost, and is found. *(resume embrace)*

Director: *(after a moment)* Cut. *(pause)* That's a wrap. Let's get some lunch.

Father: *(to congregation):* Speaking of lunch, the Father's had his servants prepare another feast for his wayward daughters and sons. Our Lord's the host; you're the honored guest.

— Exeunt —

Scripture Index

MARK WM. RADECKE is pastor of Christ Lutheran Church, Roanoke, Virginia. He is Adjunct Professor of Religion at Roanoke College, Salem, Virginia. He graduated from the University of Maryland with a degree in Theatre and Speech and from the Lutheran Theological Seminary at Gettysburg. He is the author of several published sermons and book reviews. A native of Baltimore, Radecke is married to Lee and the father of Jessica and Christopher.

"THERE IS NO preexistent mold into which the subtance of thought must be poured in order to make a sermon." So says H. Grady Davis in the introduction to this creative volume. Like Davis, Mark Radecke is convinced preaching ought to take as many creative shapes as possible. Why should the preacher lock him or her self into a deadly rut when there exist possibilities as varied as Montage, Vignette, Allegory, Letter, Extended Illustration and Chancel Drama? **IN MANY VARIOUS WAYS** provides sterling examples of ten creative alternatives to ordinary discourse which the imaginative parish pastor can use as idea-prodding models for a richer preaching style. A Scripture index is included.

5806 / ISBN 0-89536-721-1   The C.S.S. Publishing Company, Inc.

O8-DHN-336